SNAKES

COPPERHEADS

James E. Gerholdt
ABDO & Daughters

Published by Abdo & Daughters, 4940 Viking Drive, Suite 622, Edina, Minnesota 55435.

Library bound edition distributed by Rockbottom Books, Pentagon Tower, P.O. Box 36036, Minneapolis, Minnesota 55435.

Printed in the United States.

Cover Photo credit: James Gerholdt
Interior Photo credits: Peter Arnold, Inc. pages 7, 9, 13, 17, 21

James Gerholdt, pages 5, 11, 15, 19

Edited by Julie Berg

Library of Congress Cataloging-in-Publication Data

Gerholdt, James E., 1943
  Copperheads / James E. Gerholdt.
  p. cm. — (Snakes)
Includes bibliographical references (p. 24) and index.
Summary: Describes the physical characteristics, habitat, food habits, and defense mechanisms of this poisonous pit viper.
ISBN 1-56239-514-9
1. Copperheads—Juvenile literature. [1. Copperheads. 2. Poisonous snakes. 3. Snakes.] I. Title. II. Series: Gerholdt, James E., 1943- Snakes.
QL666.069G47   1995
597.96—dc20
                                                  95-9047
                                                    CIP
                                                      AC

About the Author

Jim Gerholdt has been studying reptiles and amphibians for more than 40 years. He has presented lectures and displays throughout the state of Minnesota for 9 years. He is a founding member of the Minnesota Herpetological Society and is active in conservation issues involving reptiles and amphibians in India and Aruba, as well as Minnesota.

Contents

COPPERHEADS

Copperheads belong to one of the 11 families of snakes. They are divided into five **subspecies**.

Snakes are **reptiles**, which are **vertebrates**. This means they have a backbone, just like a human.

Copperheads are **cold blooded**. They get their body temperature from lying in the sun or on a warm rock or the warm ground. If they are too cool, their bodies won't work. If they get too hot, they will die.

These snakes are called copperheads because of their coppery-red colored heads.

*You can see the coppery-red head on
this broad-banded copperhead.*

SIZES

Copperheads are medium sized snakes and are very heavy bodied. The copperhead's length is measured from the tip of the nose to the tip of the tail. Each **subspecies** is a different size.

The smallest copperhead is the Trans-Pecos copperhead. It is 20 to 30 inches (51 to 76 cm) in length. The record size for this snake is only 32 7/8 inches (83.5 cm).

The largest copperhead is the northern copperhead. It is 24 to 36 inches (61 to 91 cm) in length. The record for this snake is 4.4 feet (1.3 m). This is the largest size ever recorded for any of the five copperheads.

The smallest copperhead is the Trans-Pecos.
It measures 20 to 30 inches (51 to 76 cm) long.

COLORS

Copperheads are very brightly colored. Their bodies range from pinkish in color to a gray brown.

There are a series of brown to reddish-brown markings, called **saddles**, along the back. These saddles are broader near the belly and narrower on the back of the snake. The tail is yellow, brown, or green, and is especially bright on the babies.

The belly of a copperhead is pink, light brown, or cream colored with darker blotches on the outside areas. Each copperhead type has different colors and saddle shapes.

This northern copperhead has a coppery-red head and a brown body.

WHERE THEY LIVE

Copperheads are found in different **habitats**. The northern copperhead likes wooded hillsides with rock crevices or rock piles. The southern copperhead likes low ground near swamps or streams with **cypress** trees. The Osage copperhead likes both types of habitats.

The broad-banded copperhead likes wooded areas with a thick layer of oak leaves. The Trans-Pecos copperhead is found near springs and streams in west Texas. It will sometimes find its way into the nearby desert areas. Each copperhead has its own place in the world.

The southern copperhead likes low ground near swamps or streams with cypress trees.

WHERE THEY ARE FOUND

Each copperhead has its own **habitat** in the United States. Only the Trans-Pecos copperhead is found in the Mexican states of Chihuahua and Coahuila along the Texas border.

The broad-banded copperhead is found in Texas and Oklahoma (OK). The Osage copperhead lives in Oklahoma, Arkansas (AR), Missouri (MO), Kansas (KS), southeastern Nebraska (NE), Iowa (IA), and eastern Illinois (IL).

**The broad-banded copperhead is found in
Texas and Oklahoma.**

The southern copperhead ranges across the southern
United States from Texas eastward. The northern
copperhead is found from Texas to Massachusetts (MA)
and Connecticut (CT).

SENSES

Copperheads and humans share four of the same senses. They have trouble seeing anything that isn't moving.

Their pupils are **vertical** to help them see better in the dark, where much of their activity takes place. These vertical pupils open up in the dark to let in more light.

Like all snakes, copperheads have no ears and cannot hear. They can feel **vibrations** through bones in the lower jaw.

Smell is the snakes most important sense. All snakes use their tongue with which to smell.

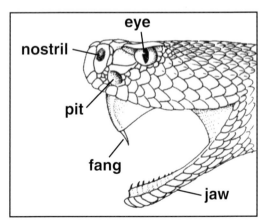

You can see the tongue and one of the heat-sensing pits on this broad-banded copperhead.

Copperheads have two heat-sensing pits between the mouth and nostrils that help them find warm-blooded **prey**. This is why they are also called **pit vipers**.

DEFENSE

Though they are brightly colored, copperheads blend in with their surroundings. This is called **camouflage**. It is their most important defense against their enemies.

If an enemy can't see it, the copperhead is safe. But if an enemy does find it, or is about to step on it, the snake will shake its tail.

Though there is no rattle on the tail, it will sound like one when the snake is in dry leaves or grass. The copperhead will also spray a smelly liquid on an enemy.

If none of these defenses work, the copperhead will simply strike and bite. The fangs are long and can **inject venom** into the enemy. Although it is seldom deadly to a human, it is very painful!

Copperheads blend into their surroundings. This is called camouflage and is the best defense against enemies.

FOOD

Copperheads will eat just about any type of animal it can swallow. Like all snakes, they only eat other animals. Snakes do not eat fruits or vegetables.

A small copperhead will eat insects, frogs, lizards, snakes, and small turtles. Larger copperheads eat birds and small **mammals**. Young copperheads will sometimes use their bright yellow tail to lure frogs within striking distance.

The different copperheads have their favorite food. But all copperheads use their **venom** to kill animals for food.

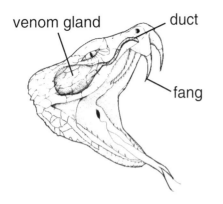

venom gland   duct

fang

Venom is made in the venom glands. The glands are on both sides of the snake's head and lie outside the main jaw muscles toward the back of the head. When the snake bites, the venom travels from each gland through the ducts and the hollow fangs, and into the prey.

Copperheads eat just about anything they can swallow whole. This broad-banded copperhead is eating a mouse.

BABIES

Copperheads give birth to live young. The female can have one to twenty babies. They average four to eight.

The baby copperheads are 7.5 to 11 inches (19 to 28 cm) in length. The size and number of the young depend on the size of the female.

After the babies are about seven to ten days old, they shed their skin for the first time. After the skin has been shed, the babies are ready to hunt their food.

As the snakes grow, they will shed their skin whenever the old skin gets too small. A baby will shed several times in a year. An adult will shed only once a year.

This is a female southern copperhead with her newborn babies.

GLOSSARY

Camouflage (CAM-a-flaj) - The ability to blend in with the surroundings.

Cold-blooded - Gaining body temperature from an outside source.

Cypress (SY-press) - An evergreen tree with small, dark leaves like scales.

Habitat (HAB-uh-tat) - An area in which an animal lives.

Inject - To force liquid into the body through fangs.

Mammal - Warm-blooded animals with a backbone and usually have hair that feed their young milk.

Pit vipers - Snakes with heat-sensing pits.

Prey - An animal that is hunted for food.

Reptile (REP-tile) - A scaly-skinned animal with a backbone.

Saddles (SAD-dells) - Markings narrower at the top than at the bottom.

Subspecies - A geographic race of a species.

Venom - Snake poison that is used to kill animals for food.

Vertical (VERT-i-cul) - Up and down.

Vertebrate (VER-tuh-brit) - An animal with a backbone.

Vibration (Vie-BRAY-shun) - A quivering or trembling motion.

Index

BIBLIOGRAPHY

Conant, Roger and Joseph T. Collins. *A Field Guide to Reptiles and Amphibians of Eastern and Central North America* - Third Edition. Houghton Mifflin Company, 1991.

Ernst, Carl H. and Roger W. Barbour. *Snakes of Eastern North America.* George Mason University Press, 1989.

Tennant, Alan. *A Field Guide to the Snakes of Texas.* Texas Monthly Press, *1985.*
————.*The Snakes of Texas.* Texas Monthly Press, 1984.